Cloud Camera

Lesley Saunders is the author of several books and pamphlets of poetry, including *Christina the Astonishing* (with Jane Draycott and artist Peter Hay) and *Her Leafy Eye* (with artist Geoff Carr), both published by Two Rivers Press. Lesley's work has been widely published in journals and anthologies, and has won major awards, including the Manchester Poetry Prize 2008. She has held several poetry residencies and had commissions to commemorate special occasions or themes; she is also involved in ongoing collaborations with artists and dancers.

By the same author:

The Dark Larder, Corridor Press (1997)

Christina the Astonishing, with Jane Draycott and Peter Hay,
   Two Rivers Press (1998)

Her Leafy Eye, a collaboration with artist Geoff Carr, Two Rivers
   Press (2009)

No Doves, Mulfran Press (2010)

Some Languages Are Hard To Dream In, with artist Christopher
   Hedley-Dent, Mulfran Press (2010)

Also by Two Rivers Poets:

Paul Bavister, *Miletree* (1996)

Paul Bavister, *Glass* (1998)

Paul Bavister, *The Prawn Season* (2002)

Kate Behrens, *The Beholder* (2012)

Adrian Blamires, *The Effect of Coastal Processes* (2005)

Adrian Blamires, *The Pang Valley* (2010)

Joseph Butler, *Hearthstone* (2006)

Jane Draycott and Lesley Saunders, *Christina the Astonishing* (1998)

Jane Draycott, *Tideway* (2002)

John Froy, *Eggshell: A Decorator's Notes* (2007)

David Greenslade, *Zeus Amoeba* (2009)

A. F. Harrold, *Logic and the Heart* (2004)

A. F. Harrold, *Postcards from the Hedgehog* (2007)

A. F. Harrold, *Flood* (2009)

Ian House, *Cutting the Quick* (2005)

Gill Learner, *The Agister's Experiment* (2011)

Kate Noakes, *The Wall Menders* (2009)

Tom Phillips, *Recreation Ground* (2012)

Victoria Pugh, *Mrs Marvellous* (2008)

Peter Robinson, *English Nettles and Other Poems* (2010)

Peter Robinson (ed.), *Reading Poetry: An Anthology* (2011)

Peter Robinson (ed.), *A Mutual Friend: Poems for Charles Dickens* (2012)

Susan Utting, *Houses Without Walls* (2006)

Susan Utting, *Fair's Fair* (2012)

Cloud Camera

Lesley Saunders

TWO
RIVERS
PRESS

First published in the UK in 2012 by Two Rivers Press
7 Denmark Road, Reading RG1 5PA.
www.tworiverspress.com

ISBN 978-1-901677-81-2

British Library Cataloguing in Publication Data. A catalogue record
for this book is available from the British Library.

1 2 3 4 5 6 7 8 9

Two Rivers Press is represented in the UK by Inpress Ltd and
distributed by Central Books.

Cover design and illustration by Sally Castle.
Text design by Nadja Guggi and typeset in Janson and Parisine.

Printed and bound in Great Britain by Imprint Digital, Exeter.

For my family

Acknowledgements

Thanks are due to the editors of the following journals, magazines, anthologies and websites who first published some of the poems in this book, including the Bridport Prize Anthology 2011, the Cardiff International Poetry Competition website 2011, the *Days of Roses* website, *Divers*, *Domestic Cherry*, the English Association Newsletter, the Hippocrates Prize Anthology 2011, the Manchester Poetry Prize website 2008, *Mslexia*, *Poetry News*, *The Rialto*, *The Rules of Form*, *The Warwick Review*, *Upstart*.

A number of the poems – 'A Hare's Breath', 'Cloud Camera', 'Comet Sweeper', 'Glass', 'Globe', 'Moon Landing', 'Organ', 'Sunshine Recorder', 'Tremor' and 'Warbler' – were inspired by exhibits at the Whipple Museum of the History of Science, Cambridge. I am accordingly most grateful to Kelley Swain, poet in residence at the Whipple, for arranging for me to give a first reading of these poems at the museum in July 2011.

I should also like to thank the President and Fellows of Murray Edwards College (formerly New Hall), Cambridge, for awarding me a visiting scholarship to create a poetry project around the college gardens in 2008–09: 'Cob Oven', 'Dark Matter', 'Remains' and 'Tender Exotics' are from the resulting sequence of poems.

My thanks are also due to Adrian Blamires, Allison McVety, Hilda Sheehan and members of the Poetry Workshop for their comments on earlier versions of some of the poems; and most especially to Helen McNeil and Bridget Somekh for their invaluable advice on the collection as a whole.

Contents

III. Far Objects

Last night I discovered a comet near 1st (∂) Ophiuchi, but clouds covering the part of the heavens where it was, its place could not be obtained.

— Caroline Herschel, letter to Joseph Planta, Secretary of the Royal Society, 8 October 1793

I. Dark Matter

Organ

the human can be taken apart and reassembled.
— Papier-mâché anatomical model designed by Dr Louis Auzoux

Apparently I am made of parts. A locked box of troubles,
a walled town always on the brink of plague, rebellion,
a mediaeval sunless place of chopped rags and powdered cork
held together with flour-paste, then gesso-painted

to look real; the attention to detail is breathtaking.
This set of female pieces is especially useful for students,
it diagnoses a human womb in the gothic of pregnancy,
disclosing the little male tucked inside like the very last doll

or a silent growth: the wire nerves, red-ribbon veins, relentless
panorama of follies. See, these lobotomies and hysterectomies
are mendable, their vivid jigsaws like slipper orchids leave
nothing to the imagination. But behind my skirts

I am unlit rooms, a visionary anatomy shaken by small fevers.
How I live is dark science, fretful fugue; a mirror under a shawl.

Medicine Chest

Bearing the marks of use acquired during these heroic undertakings …

As the plane bucks in over the mountains
I screw the top off a little bottle of white rioja
and hold on my tongue a Latin prophylactic

ora pro nobis till it dissolves and we land.
It took me three weeks to pack, as many days
as my mission lasts, all the blister-packs

of nostrums for night-frights and the vertigo
I get in glass-bottomed lifts. The apartment
reeks of smoke, the particulate air of capital cities,

its electrics aren't earthed, the tap-water smells
of bad eggs. I do not find the river's source or
give it my name; I wedge the door with a chair

before bed. Each day is a small wooden drawer
in which I look for cures. The portable ache of self.

Progeny

*Dreamt that my little baby came to life again; that it had only
been cold, and that we rubbed it before the fire, and it lived.*
— Mary Shelley, *Journals*

I re-pack my suitcase, its phantom contents spilling
   over the edge of the bed, unrecognisably mine but

with the moonlight struggling through and a sense
   of the glassy lake and high white Alps beyond

like a pile of stricken photos. Something red and silky
   in the middle of the room refuses to be folded,

but she's not man enough, it's not hers to make life
   out of used words. Faces rise through the waves,

a jumble of coloured-in skulls, experimentations
   in animal magnetism, time travel, that I must re-arrange

in the order they came in. This is no writer's block,
   it's in the blood as deep as mother and child,

the subject is conscious, stepping out warm into life.
   Then the dearness of the dream vanishes, there was just

a ship trapped in a sea of ice, the paper it was printed on.

Experiment

Electricity was the craze of the eighteenth century ...
— Paola Bertucci, *Sparks in the Dark*, 2007

Nearly everything must be invented, about the boy or boys who
took part:
whether the parents gave their consent, whether friends were
envious
or scared, how unexpectedly their dreams of flying would end –
though

you'd know the moment you'd met one by the excitable wings of
his collar,
by the folded ailerons of the shoulder-blades, the way his
uncertain hair
had coiled itself into wires, and the eyes like skies after
lightning. Even so,

hearing a series of small storms in a room upstairs, you'd hardly
infer
what was there. Something suspended, clairvoyant, a body of
evidence
plying between laws of desire and repulsion, results and their
cause,

the child all the while sparkling, a lark-mirror, a dark chandelier,
levitating
feathers, confetti, gritty leaves of gold that fill his nose and
mouth like a shout,
till he's an ariel in the bird-catcher's hand, thrilled almost to
bits.

What makes it work is the silk, and the virtue repeatedly applied
to his heels:
hinting, if only the rain holds off, at brave new systems for
travelling through time
over wild-eyed distances, high wire acts over oceans and prairies,
a rodeo of lights.

For some looking back it must have seemed just a dream, a phrase
they'd been
going through, unconditional and perfect; for others, a warning
of danger to come,
charged, resistant, different: a world spun by a whisker, the future
before it's begun.

The New Look

horse-(chariots), painted crimson and with joinery work complete,
supplied with reins. The rail(?) is of fig-wood, with fittings(?) of horn,
and there is (no?) 'heel'(?)
— Linear B tablet

There had just been a war and in its wake
came glamour, cinch-waisted, gloved and hatted;
up and down the land the soft scrape
of tailor's pins on tissue, tiny stencils of sound

as women and their apprentice-daughters knelt
to their guesswork: barathea organza jacquard poplin,
reading in the dots and dashes darts back-half-belts
seven-eighths sleeves side-vents double-peplums,

while dragons' teeth sprang up in the aftermath.
The trick was turning the chiffon or buffalo
carefully round on the needle or shoulder of earth
goading garments or armour into eye-catching poses,

greek still being a classical affair very vogue
very english, glaphyròs and taffeta to mid-calf,
when suddenly out of a new-fangled past a brogue
blew in like a bare-arsed ruffian *ka-ko to-ra-ke ko-ru*,

his grey clay of man-verbs threatening a landslide
of glottals stuffed in the throats of foot-soldiers
holing out in some tora bora on rations of flies
and dry winds through an age of iron and thunder:

all the war-words that had been trying like utility frocks
run up from parachute-cloth to forget themselves
and what they stood for, all those lives, times, locked
tightly in, writing with no reading, all key-words in hiding.

There had been a war, or soon would be again,
another lingo to go missing in action or awol
its shot silks and syllables left out in the sing-song rain
all greek no cribs no titles just these tiny stencils of sound.

A Person is not a Landscape

As always, it's the hills that impress me, their bare mauve cones
and the wisps of high cirrus hanging about like old smoke

though I notice my colleagues prefer to turn the other way
towards the endless renewing of sea and sky, the view over the bay.

I remember we clinked as we trod, trowels and steel rods
imprinting our soft pockets, swifts dinking over our heads,

the turbines of midges, an occasional white sparkle off the stones
as we rootled in ditches, listening for the tap or scrape of the unknown

yet also, I think, unwilling to imagine the mountain leaping out of its
  skin,
the trees turning the silver backs of their leaves to the burning wind.

Most of the gold had gone; what else was there under the rubble and
  ash?
(We'd heard a whole statuette had been gentled up from beneath the
  crush.)

In time, I confess, it came to obsess me. What kind of space is a person,
what shape is made in the air by her passions, prayers, reasons?

We poured plaster into the wounds of the city, watching while it
  congealed
until we could see the shapes people made in the tuff like hares in a
  field:

the shallow platters of their bellies, the calderas of their breasts,
the elegant arcades of their legs, the meditational hoods of their heads,

the lipped ceramics of their ears, the locked cabinets of their chests,
the peripateias of their elbows, the lotuses of their wrists,

the exhortations of their arms pulling each other closer,
the heavenly domes of their eyelids, the last refuges of their toes.

Their bodies (what else could I call them?) became a dead, leaden white,
their clothing and skin bled a stale darkness into the day's stark light

and I began to wonder, what have I done, what could it possibly mean,
if we were stealing their freedom, dreaming we'd set them free?

What was real was the cloudburst of a man's breath like a shout on his
    tongue
and the fire in the mountain that put itself out in his lungs.

World

The forming and breaking-up of supercontinents appears
to be cyclical throughout Earth's 4.6 billion year history ...
— Wikipedia

after the sculpture 'Sleeping Landscape' by Kate Nottage

Along the shining coastline of my arm
my skull lies ungardened, my sleep is granite,
obsidian. I'm drifting north of Utsire

into the far greys of ocean, I can feel
my knees spreading polished and wingless
as Gondwana, I am pregnant with

newfoundlands, I shall live through aeons
of mountains until my ores of acorns
and gold are exhausted, and I die

an old woman, the trade winds
of my breathing congealing to ice-floes
and snow-geese. Only in dreams

am I burning, turning to salamanders
and murder, born again as furnace,
as fire-in-the-heart, a treacle of hungry glass.

Mad Music

*If Chimes could whisper, if Melodies could pass away, and their souls
wander the Earth … if Ghosts danced at Ghost Ridottoes, 'twould require
such Musick, Sentiment ever held back, ever at the edge of breaking forth,
in Fragments, as Glass breaks.*
— Thomas Pynchon, *Mason & Dixon*, 1997

It's a symphony of would-be smithereens
composed of the coveted see-through stuff
that glaziers tweeze into xylophones

or eyes, though the ring of it is a spill
of semitones over a weir, its bleak
brilliant cadences rhyme with pure,

with sheer, as if the icicles of the moon,
its sharp-eyed hills and sitka spruces
have guessed their vitreous names,

the brittle way to say them, as if you
alone have heard the steepling voices
a city sings in from its high bright ledges,

whilst all the time your mind is falling falling
through a million sheet-glass malls.

Sphaerotheca Pannosa

I am soft as a mouse and tiny-quiet,
creeping in under the eye
of the moon through the harvest days.

By morning you will be wearing me
like a fur, a velvet shroud
round the fade of your flesh, my rose.

The Rose

You think fresh air, and quiet and cleanliness extravagant,
perhaps dangerous, luxuries …
— Florence Nightingale, *Notes on Nursing*, 1859

Its petals were the causes of death. In sleep
I'm sleepless with feelings of war, the soft organs
of anxiety. There are stories going the rounds,

the organised crimes of wounds and neglect,
mitigable zymotic infections, cholera, frostbite.
It's women's work, washing and feeding the men,

collecting clinical data from vast fields of filth:
the rose has its own symmetry, its colours yielding
and still clear like a day in the past when something

happened or did not or should have or else
was a terrible mistake: the areas may be compared.
I cartwheel among the sheets, banner headlines

behind my shut eyes, war-paint on horseback.
The rose unfolds, deaths inching out from its midst.

Peccant Attoms

Ah Messieurs! que je vous plains! –
— Fanny Burney

This morning has its own history, it's the size of a fist,
a showcase of pain. Bonaparte is blockading the city,

at any moment the sounds of cutting will begin,
bringing the Seine to your eyes. In such conditions

the body is belligerent and vivid, a fast-moving prose:
his forefinger first described a straight line from top to bottom

of the breast, secondly a Cross, & thirdly a Circle.
There remains only the syntax of clean bandages

and, as the muscle goes under the knife, silent dictation.
Bonescraping and terror are the other verbs. Soon

anarchy will be eradicated. The seven men in black
are not a euphemism, the violence is unspeakable.

The patient survives in order to describe, her pen
is self-inflicted, surgical, like polished steel.

Laughing Gas

a degree of hilarity altogether new to me –
— Mr Coates, of Bristol

There were only minutes to go, I was on my knees
in a kind of ravishment, inhaling the amiable gas

as if a life depended on it. The room was full
of watchers yet I was taking a solitary moonlit walk

through shoeless corridors until the small hours
grew huge with euphoric light. *I suddenly lost sight*

of all the objects round me, they being apparently obscured
by clouds, in which were many luminous points.

I was rolling in the aisles, I was splitting my sides,
I was hysterical, fit to burst. Meticulous notes were taken,

but as if seen through a shine of tears, and although
next day the entire experience appeared dreamlike

I felt like the sound of a harp, I seemed a sublime being
newly created, I was ready to die laughing.

Lecture

No physician forgets his first exposure to a cadaver …
— Harvey V. Fineberg, *Visionary Anatomies*, 2005

A crowd gathers in the gallery,
shuffles as one to the front.
Bodies shift and huddle,

jammed up against each other
as intimately as the jumble of organs
slithering into view

from the cavity of the dead man
spreadeagled on the table.
This is the seat of melancholy,

here is where the bile rises;
behold the gastric wilderness,
the visceral sublime – in his guts

the events that anguished him,
bitter pap it took a lifetime to digest.
The pink snout of his appendix

nestles like a footnote, an exile
from the grand peristaltic narrative
that ran from his lips to the last

of his nine doors. If the inner life
is real, this must be it, not the weeping skies
painted inside the domes of his eyelids,

the sailcloth moons. The air has a chill
chemical smell. We try not to faint,
standing here catching our deaths.

Couch

They are all nerves, neuroses, and neurasthenia ...
— Lorenzo Stecchetti, letter to the gastronome Pellegrino Artusi, 1890

From the stomach of the unconscious
startled dream-like objects are being retrieved,
handled like antiques, given collectors' names.
After dinner he'll arrange them in a mandala
on the mirrored table-top, the saltspoons,
crucifixes, hairpins, wounds.

This is a room that knows itself, deeper than red,
Mycenean, saturated. It's a burial-ground
of obsessions: displays of inlaid eyes,
bone, ivory – flesh's spies
on the psyche, a whole-body problem
en déshabillé. A scene is being set: here

geophages and dolorous sword-swallowers
tightrope-walk across the Persian rug, watched
by bull-leapers and dog-headed gods.
Voyeurs, full of their own insights.
He has them on a leash,
like dirty words. She is stuffing the cushions

down her throat, dévoré velvets, cravings
she likes the taste of, anything crimson
that comes into her mind. Behind her head,
for a moment he's the Jewish refugee
renting a space to live, staining his beard
with nicotine. At the edges of his reverie

is a landing lit sidelong by a bay window,
a shining grey seascape taking shape inside him
like a bookcase of afternoons.
Then he remembers where he is, downstairs
with the curtains drawn, the closed eyelids
of his patient, the mute wolfed things.

Remains

Under the tennis courts a mirabelle orchard,
  under the orchard cables and rubble,

remnants of human settlement labelled or guessed at,
  a cow-skull laid facing west, later floodwater

soiling the day-room. DNA under the fingernails.
  What I recall is the storm, the downpour

through whose cathedral I hurtled in bare feet,
  the rain through my frock like a hot second skin.

Soon they would leave, carrying the scrolls and god-things
  out of the burning, the fire and smoke of autumn,

the leaf-soot, leaf-brittle, forgotten laundry,
  the ash and grist of seeds, shoes in the car park.

I, we, three, the oldest words in English.
  Remembering changes how things were.

The Classification of Clouds

Clouds are ... as good visible indicators of the operation of these causes [of atmospheric change], as is the countenance of the state of a person's mind or body.
— Luke Howard, *Essay on the Modification of Clouds,* 1803

The photographs are reliable: I have English weathers,
they show on my face
like the uncertainties of summer (the coolest
in how many years, cumulonimbus sitting on the roof
thundery as a month of pigeons). This one
would have me confessing to murder,
my expression resists grace endlessly. Or,

letting go of the old, I might have lifted my eyes
on an unlikely opening, a spectrum of empty colours
only a dedicated colourist could achieve. Clouds
defy the line, they will not be penned or pencilled,
they fly and free-associate above my landscape
whose only purpose is painting skies,
grey, greyer, greyest,

trying again and again to make it so. Then blue.
I am flat on my back. Long-sighted
with age, looking more like my mother,
I stare at the ceiling for signs of the holy ghost,
rosy-fleshed paraclete, in these unstable episodes.
Everything is connected. The alp going up
in red smoke, the lake flooding itself with flame

– you never know when you wake what you'll face,
whether the opposite shore will be visible
from where you stand at the wave-watcher's window
a manic-depressive distillation of mist
amassing between the domains of gold and dirt.
It's all classifiable. There are names, Latin. Signs of human
damage. Trees on the point of disappearing from view.

In the Realm of Dreams, the Alter Ego is Master

In August 1909, while lunching with Jung at a restaurant in Bremen,
Freud suddenly fainted; in November 1912, at a psychoanalytic
conference in Munich, Freud fainted again while Jung was speaking –
Jung carried him to a couch …

It was an ottoman, covered in silk-weave kilims, heavy-set
and generous like a lake whose main darkness is off-shore,
unmoored and so openly reminiscent of the body's
need to dream. Shouldered by removers into the day-room
where rivers feed the marinas and promenade-gardens,

it had about it an aura of absence, a lifetime of mourning,
it was a lost world where light gathered, grey as a pearl,
just above the fast-swimming clouds. Like lake-shore walkers
or coded self-portraits two men appeared to be resting, one asleep,
the other looking out towards the mountain. Much was unsaid,

the last war still fresh in the memory, some ills beyond help
so soon afterwards. Talking was impossible even to oneself –
behind a wall a string quartet was rehearsing its camouflage
music. The faint had lasted only a few seconds but it was draped
in scarlet like a too-warm room, a fatherland of tall-plumed hats:

all over Europe the guardians of instinct were taking their leave.
Decades after, Gustav and Schlomo, made fretful by forgetfulness,
palpitations, poor digestion, have met to take a final meal together
– though these days nothing tastes as it should, even repentance.
They shake hands, feeling the other's grip. This will be a fight

with shadows, they are old women with breasts and crows'-feet,
nearly unrecognisable as the Glee and Young of former years: watch
how the one helps the other to sit, easing him onto the banquette.
The beak-faced waiters can barely hide their impatience.
Armer Konrad, poor Conrad, for whom Herr Doktor has no cure.

Heberden's Nodes

*Pretend that you're drawing your arms through water, and you're leaving
a soft, rippling trail from your wrists to your fingertips –*
— How to Place Hands in Ballet

These are the corals my bones have made,
their skeletal sea-changes.
Under my fingers' skin,

on the distal interphalangeal joints
of my toes,
the spiny reefs are forming,

knuckled fastnesses
for angel fish
and the static ballet of anemones.

My wrists do not dance
that Balanchine way they used to,
the air pooling round them

and the thumb supple
as a frond;
small shoals of sharp-finned

pains swim between eroded bone salt
and cartilage.
Lifting my bare foot, the doctor

puts it on his knee, the warmth
of his palms
a thoughtful poultice,

his diagnosis a close watch kept
at centuries of bedsides
while I am turning to sculpture

in the good physician's name
– calcareous, spurred,
like flowers of iron.

Thrombus

So, as he said, the key to it all
is the rhythm, the walking uphill,

the steps in the wall, the knock
in the blood, the knocking on wood

which is the pumping of sap, the sob
in the heart or sump of the forest

unlocking the roots, releasing the green.
And, as he said, it is also a matter of flow:

how we monitor the breathing
by our own mornings and evenings

and suddenly when it's in danger
of stopping, so we can work to insert a stent

or whole stanza of air like a prayer for mercy,
the daily psalms of statin and aspirin –

and listening hear the pulse again like a verse,
and watching see the look on the face

of someone coming round from a dream.

The Narrow Road to the Interior

Before enlightenment, fetch wood, carry water. After enlightenment,
fetch wood, carry water.
— Zen Proverb

for LG

You said a calligrapher of the old school
would spend a lifetime to make a single line,

with which he could feel not pleased
but that he had made the journey somewhere

and seen it for himself – the misty rain
on Mount Ro or the incoming tide at Sekk ,

let us imagine. You said it would be the last
twenty-four hours of your known world,

that one of your breasts would be English,
the other American, a new wild geography

to live in, as if you had been waiting these years
to go dancing there. And I think of you now

dressed in red; and of *'the grace of a woman*
going out with a lamp to light her way'.

II. Voyagers

The Fallen Angels

the sciences … were originally taught by the fallen angels.
— C. G. Jung, *Answer to Job,* 1952

for Richard Holmes

They experimented on themselves, no longer believing
in god's perfect-circle certitudes. Not knowing limits,
they had to invent them – what the terrestrial body can stand,
at what point the mind turns itself inside out. Those heads,

those shrunken leathers shovelled up from peat-bogs, rotting,
are they theirs, that we looked on with awe and revulsion?
Was it from these we got the base metals of our earth, the art
of working them, the propagation of root-cuttings, or the beautifying

of the eyelids, the classification of clouds, not to be unlearned now?
Were these the blue riders, with their riot of colours storming
our law-abiding dreams? Were they the spectacle-makers,
the lens-grinders conjuring visions, with their mirrors did we watch

the death of stars? Accepting only the testimony of our own eyes,
did we spy the spark leap the roseless void, its split-second
life of violence? Have we tested it all yet to destruction?
Shall we sail with them the longitudes to Otaheite, hunting souls?

The Emperor's Mother Has Delusions

I sit still and invisible
behind the quilted silk
in the innermost room
of the Great Within
where only your ministers
seeking audience may tread
in cotton slippers
on the lacquered floor
that reflects their petticoats

but I know they know
I see and hear many things

– do you not hear it, my son,
the soft whirring of the machine
that came bandaged in linen
carted over a winter and summer
of deserts and through all the houses
of the zodiac from the city they say
floats on a bowl of sea, whose palaces
are bright as rice lanterns, whose
women are monster-footed?

Its intricate little tines and springs
have more tricks than the new concubine
I've been feeding on musk.
But its fifty clicking wheels presume
to bear the weight of our imperial days
that were once dense with computations
of jasmine: it has gone hunting
in the heavens, this thing they call
a clock, and caged the sun.

My son, the great walls
of our eternity are breached,
do you not see?

The scents of time passing
are no longer sweet and
the end of wisdom has begun.

Tremor

Midi: grande silence ...
— Olivier Messiaen, *Réveil des Oiseaux*

Professor Sekiya Seikei
not a violent man
removes his shoes
and twists a hank of metal
like obi ribbon.

All that remains
is a cuckoo
very far away
very faint
on Asiatic woodblocks
which the composer
has marked
in his notebook
with a calligraphy
of two long silences –

the one bleached
as the stove-in hull
of an upturned boat
out there
in the city of water,

the other
offering no resistance
to sunlight
but harping on
at the broken edge of things

The faultline crosses
a garden between
two persimmon trees
and the aftershocks continue
like wind
like thunder.

The Book of Great Explorers

being a full account of the dangerous voyages, admirable adventures,
notable discoveries, and magnanimous atchievments: revised, corrected,
inlarged, and beautified with pictures –
— Sr Francis Drake Reviv'd, 1692

The routes the old explorers took are strung out in looping
dots and dashes across the pages' phosphorescent oceans

like hotel facades along the promenade seen from two miles out
as twilight dulls the rocks and flocks of gulls catch the cracked

chords of the Belle Vue band tuning up its crowds, or like those
    strands
of fancy lights laced through avenues of evening-scented tamarinds

that flash a rackety fanfare over the bay for saints' days or another
safe home-coming to the dancing lamps of ferries, oyster fairs:

as if these reckless paths might have dared to meet and cross and
    part
one far pacific night, all hands on deck, and waving tiny rusted
    lanterns

as the tall ships majestically pass, their cargo of consequences
    engulfing the dark.

Globe

Pocket Terrestrial and Celestial Globe. Inscribed Darton and Co. 1809.
Simulated fishskin case lined with celestial gores. (Valued in 2010 at £5,900.)

I was always an only child. Reading the Children's Encyclopaedia
I knew the Hittites and Hottentots were just an atlas away,

that the Eastern steppes were wonder-tales of mare's-milk, mazurkas,
that the robber girl kept a knife in her furs, that if I went far enough

I could return to where I am now. My grandmother ironing silver
sweet-papers flat with her thumbnail, willow warbler another bird

my grandfather taught me. O solemn temples and cigarette cards!
The one thing of his was a small pocket globe with a hooked catch

keeping the two halves of the cosmos closed, the dark reef
of New Holland lying under the long coasts of Australia. Or

I could have held it in one hand, made the wrinkled earth-apple
turn in the burnished bowl of its heavens. I was reading

the Reader's Digest, where it pays to increase your word-power,
but what the world was worth is a riddle I couldn't imagine.

Red Sky in the Morning

Red sky in the morning,
one crow flying alone,
two round moons in a month.
Another squall in the Bay of Biscay,
another wild goose chase,
the sound of torn canvas
like the tatter of wing-beats
on thin air.

Behind sun-splashed windows
admirals shuffle their papers:
'systems save lives,
we demand a law of storms,
cumulus et nimbus,
plain as the nose, as day follows –
not this moonshine and old wives,
this blathering and dithering
while our ships go down
in the maelstrom, a sleet
of lost souls.'

Red sky at night. Along the shore
a diligent navy of observers
fans out from Margate noticing
the way the brassy light lifts
the whole sea on its back, how
the wavelets go slick and black
as china ink, and a slight breeze,
out-breath of nightfall, can be felt
on the hairs of their arms.

The mercury levitates in FitzRoy's glass,
trawlers bob like gulls on the swell
yellow-eyed in the dusk,
herring-hungry, and are home
safe at dawn.

This voyage will be a test, a forecast
of more than the weather, he'll need
a companion to sail all the way
with his soul to the stone-cold ends
of the earth to the shattered beginnings
of time, the twin he's been waiting for,
absent since birth.

Darwin's consulting the timetable
of rocks, his bible of begats
and bequests, loathe to believe
what he believes he can see.
His captain takes another sounding,
copperplates some numerals
just off the cape, unable to fathom
the grim-faced tortoises who know
in their bones which way the wind
blows, their slow morphologies
of surviving.

Red sky at night. The ship rides
in the mist, hypothetical, almost
extinct, like a tempest of words
that have blown themselves out
on a galapagos of facts. Something
not lost has been found.

Red sky in the morning. A village
teetering for a week on a wave-eaten
cliff floats like scripture in the sky
then in bedside tables gravestones cutlery
tumbles the fossils of itself
along the beach.

Red sky in the morning, and the man
who was captain wakes with the sense
of nothing under his feet. Just the slow
trapeze of thoughts and days, a leakage
of faith as if he'd opened a vein, as if
he was all at sea.

The New Guns

Celandines gloss the mud in Totland's rutted streets,
morning's bright with windows stalking sun,
housemaids lean saucily from casements,
barracking the big lads, the gun-busters, whose sweat
drips on their boots as they muscle, twelve to a crew,
twenty eight tons of rifled steel towards the cliff.

La Gloire dips and heaves in mutual seas, bold
as iron plate can make her: France
has nosed ahead in the arms race, Palmerston's
getting nervous of the Russians. 'Open your windows!
They're testing the guns!' A laundress claps hands
to ears, children to lap, calming the collie,
shushing the hens. Studded shells ride up their grooves
gathering spin. Walls and cliffs give back thunder
to the sergeant's useless ears, youths holler for more,
glassmakers smear molten faces, listening
for tomorrow's business. Missiles dent the waves
five miles away, the ordnance art's grand impress.
Huzza! the guns are true.

At the Needles, men wear calico boots.
The magazine's dusted with gunpowder:
only pussy-footing's safe. A delicate peace rests
on quivering transoms. 'We must buttress our defences!'
roars Lord Palmerston: Spithead, Dover, Thames.
Every dockyard's at full stretch, always one step
behind, artillery-led: at the ready, Messrs Palliser,
Moncrieff, Armstrong, Buffington, Clerk!
We must brace ourselves for when the Frenchies come,
no peace *sans* strength!

Concrete and granite grace downlands' swerve
to beach; turrets and tunnels, cupolas and casemates
impart design to naïve dishevelled crags:
Gibraltar, Malta, Bosphorus.

Peace lasts till war's declared. The Totland guns?
Oh, the soldier boys have gone, the story's tired:
the guns were obsolete as soon as fired.

The Invention of Night Writing

Because the small hours belong to insomniacs
spying on your soul inside its tent

Because the least of your ambitions can be lip-read
and your tactics have become the answer rather than the question

Because the blue indistinct shadows cast by the moon
are not the innocent wolves of this forest nor their hunters

Because the sound-surround of the mountains
and the echo-chamber of the lake are also your foes

Because your men are as jumpy as a duchess with an English lover
and your emperor has required it of you

Because tomorrow, though always tomorrow, you will be able
to telegraph, and later, but only later, cable and radio

Because you possess a marksman's instinct for where
the skin is thinnest, how to lift the siege of the actual

Because your fingertips have managed to remember all that is
forensic, intimate, reptilian, all that is best kept in the dark

Because soon it will come in a flash, a momentary flinch
of the flesh, a trick of the light, a pin through a map –

Because, as you put out the lamp, you can feel the words blister
and bud, the seeds of a future where even a blind man can read.

Saladin

When the end came, it was out of sight
though several minds' eyes saw it

or thought so. Sea-clouds were cave walls
scrawled all over with messages

if only someone could have broken the code.
(*The balloon is lightheaded*

with hope, holding the man in its car
like treasure or a memory

of childhood, a Sunday School outing.)
A reward was offered, the search

by coastguards and boats in the Channel
went on through the night. *The Courier*

advised readers of sightings south of the Needles
of a coal or comet alight in the sky:

a person had climbed a mountain in Spain
for the view. No trace of wreckage,

though sandbags would eventually be found
and misunderstood on private land.

(*The balloon, its basket packed with a hamper,*
plaid rugs, maps and charts of the tides,

some kind of fire extinguisher, a large thermos
of tea, became an O of astonishment

as it patrolled whole kingdoms deep in the hills,
the silver seam of a river, the stilled lakes

of ruined palaces, battlefield-tapestries stitched
with barley and flax; Albion's stone ribs.)

The breeze must have buoyed the men's shouts
upward: an unrecovered object

dropped from the balloon as it soared.
(*Five miles up*

is the zone of ice-crystals where breath
becomes visible, vision blurs

and the air freshens to steel: the balloon's
intentions are obscure but the sea

sparkles like dark matter as far
as the rim of the world.)

Moon Landing

'We went to the moon with slide rules,' said Norman Chaffee,
who worked on the spacecraft propulsion system for Apollo 11.

No bone-white moon-rays make it through this far
past the venetian blinds, the glass-fronted cabinets,
past the infra-red detectors to the baize-lined layers

of display-drawers, padlocked for the night, where
the rules are stored. Cut from boxwood, mahogany,
bakelite, plexiglass, bevelled, tongued-and-grooved,

slipsticks settle in their cases, and feel in their residual
moistures the ebb and flow of a diminutive tide
pulled by the gravity of the moon. The long haul

of its desolate dust is causing small deformations,
warpings, shrinkages, like the stirrings of an envy
in their bodies; hairlines drift a micro-millimetre

to the right or left, mantissas waver out of true.
Three billion would raise a ladder to the moon.

Astronaut's Wife

Waking again in the small hours, making tea,
walking with cupped hands into the yard
I feel your night brush my knuckles, soft and spry

as a lawn, its light sprinkle of frost dinted
with black tracks, paths ploughed by dark stars
voyaging to a pinpoint of self. Under my breath

call your name. See with your eyes the fusewire
of Amazons, lights-out of outbacks and pack-ice.
How small and puzzling our earthworks, Pentagons,

crop-marked like hill-forts on the low sierras.
Indoors I watched your grizzled shadow float
to and fro, a face in the moon. A man with your voice

slurring his words through the heat-shield. Now
the dawn's gold as grass. Our bed cold as a field.

Tender Exotics

Joseph Banks introduced to Britain a vast number of new and exotic species now regarded as native.

No fixed address and ticketless
they have taken barefoot shelter
    in the *grands jardins d'hiver*

canna, dracunculus, datura
seeking sanctuary from the winter
    of a foreign country and its rules

huddling their tropical shoulders
under gallant whiskery hopsacks
    and sucking in the humid air

like a pungent breath of home.
Spared from interrogation,
    deportation, border controls

with care they'll put down roots,
send out jasmine-scented blooms,
    their native names left unsaid,
            marooned.

Ballomania

for Myra

The actress Mrs Sage in a low-cut silk dress
is stepping into the gondola. Drifting
over St George's Field at a prodigious height,

Laetitia's been understudying Sarah Siddons
in Zara the Mourning Bride and, at a salary
of 9s. per week, is fitter to her sister Mrs Ward

of Drury Lane. Related by this marriage
to a Cheapside haberdasher and rumoured
to be sleeping with the purser of an Indiaman,

she'll sail to America with John 'Brush' Collins
and be known on her return as Mrs Robinson.
Right now she's balloon-bosomed, lighter than air,

she can hear herself living, the view is quite glorious,
all the husbands left earth-bound, gawping.

En Travesti

Drag King workshops instruct students in the manly arts of taking up space, dominating conversations, nose-picking and penis-wearing, and give them general rudeness skills.

Next on, a breeches role, the ginger-moustachio'd
Inspector-General, three-inch lifts in her shoes
and a spit-and-polish swagger for the jostling crowd.
She'll play you Piccadilly Johnny, all his little vanities,
she'll give you the brittle songs the soldiers used to sing,

she'll remind you of the times you longed to be a boy.
(More than the pretence of shoulders or the *verismo* voice,
more than the daily breast-bindings or the delicate question
of testosterone, the tell-tale jawbone, the effeminate gait,
is the control of infectious feelings, the stiff upper lip

and rock-steady hand in the death-dealing epidemic
of war, Waterloo, Crimea, Jamaica, Corfu, the fire-eaters
and smoke-machines, the hullabaloo.) Now watch her
dolled up in battledress, grand cavalry sword on her hip:
ladies, the Doctor James Barry – put your hands together, please!

A Sheep, a Duck and a Cockerel

[There were] rumours of a French airborne army invading Britain ...
the troops would fly suspended beneath hundreds of huge paper bags.

Midnight strikes and a flock of paper bags stuffed full of air
is lofted by the heat of single tea-lights. As they take to the skies
this is the only sight worth watching, the fluttering aeronautical

flames like guardian angels, secret agents, in the hawkish dark.
A cage of creatures soars tipsily above the roofs of Versailles:
we all know a man will have to be next, then the whole kit and boodle.

Captain Joe (Joseph W) Kittinger, Jr. says his prayers, steps off
and begins the twenty mile four minute freefall to earth – he can see
the extraordinary glow of its manifold atmospheres as the heaven

beneath him turns black and his ungloved right hand swells up
like a balloon. The leaves of the inflight magazine squeak a little
as I flick them over, deciding between wristwatches; ice crystals

have formed on the portholes. Looking is always an act of desire
and what he sees is the curve of a wind-blown planet streaking
towards him, its gold-rimmed clouds where the tragic weathers reside.

Yesterday the no-fly zone over Disney World was extended
sine fine, Vogue is warning 'Ditch those shimmery highlighters.'
The air is a fragile coincidence. Feel it on the high planes of your face.

III. Far Objects

Glass

I was drinking champagne, it gave me the illusion
I was made of flesh, a craze-proof, life-size model

of myself that no-one could see through. My beautiful
glass-blower's fingers were losing their lucidity, as if

at that very moment my husband were making love to me –
I imagined his minute seeds transcendent as glass bubbles

and for a second I wanted so much to be pristine and fragile
under his hands like a Blaschka jelly-fish or Chihuly supernova,

to be looked at with speculation and surrender.
It was a shattering thought. I didn't feel suicidal at the time

although it was obvious the world was going to explode,
its hyaline spores flying through the darkened museum

like a star-burst or the dismantled working parts
of the crystal Cadillac we once saw in a showroom in Bohemia.

A Hare's Breath

you ca'n't see an Elephant, properly, without a minimifying-glass
— Lewis Carroll, *Sylvie and Bruno Concluded,* 1893

Things always look larger than you remember,
   the way a dream rearranges the past, giving you

a makeshift husband, a house with jaunty rooms,
   catching the children at their most unearthly.

This is one way to summon the spirits. Or, put
   your face here till the slip of glass opens its eye

on a caber of mouse fur. The séance proceeds.
   Staring back at you is the illusion of intimacy

haloed in goldleaf, hulking and skulking, lit by stars.
   A horse-fly's sight organs are Betelgeuse

prancing in a blackened field, the rap on the table
   is the vast queue of animalcules and homunculi

pleading with you to call them by name. Oh, you
   have disturbed their sleep. Now do you believe?

Germ Theory

Hydras and Gorgons, and Chimeras dire
— William Heath, 'A Monster Soup', satirical etching of a sample
     of Thames water, 1828

We are all *sapiens*, all cherishable.
Even those of us who drink only bottled water
for fear of what's hatching in the cut-glass carafe.
Microbiology is a slow science, plenty of time
for the pigtailed bacilli of anxiety to divide and pullulate
like a saucer of leprechauns, escherichia coli, variola,
vibrio cholerae, a tsunami of golden staphylococci
pouring from the standpipe of imagination
that in hours will flood the streets with corpses:

at the Hotel Dieu a man in fancy dress
has suddenly collapsed and underneath his masque
his face is violet blue. A horrified dowager
drops her teacup – she eyes the scientist's soup
of magnified pathogens gurgling in her taps, the curdle
of volatile iodine circulating through her veins.
We wash our hands and wash our hands,
refuse ice in our summer daiquiris. On a window-ledge
little flasks of pandemonium ferment and seethe.

Dragonfly

Luminogram (cameraless photograph).
— Curtis Moffat, *Victoria & Albert Museum, c.* 1925

And then I invented two different ways
of researching the rapture of poetry: first

the psycho-phenomenological method
which captures solid bodies as light,

the other an original theoretical analysis
of the fine, almost plasmic, matter

it is made of. In both cases my work
was received with a sigh of applause

although I won no prizes. I felt
people's hands softly stroking my head,

how the radiance passed through us all,
and I flipped shut the slideshow I'd prepared:

they knew intuitively. Do you want
a map for the dark? Here are its wings.

Cloud Camera

I found an Edwardian pair of earrings, you could call it theft
or rescue, call it teardrops or an Omnicolore portrait of a lady,

an image of the whole sky inevitably appearing distorted
from whatever distance it is looked at. I do not know why

such sophisticated equipment was necessary (though clouds
can be heartbreakingly beautiful with their marquasites

and hidden childhoods, their insides of light) nor why
when I woke I felt contented in that after-rain way I remember

from our pinhole years. The edges are silvered,
foxed, enchanting despite or because of the angle of the rays

which I have no option but to call phi and theta. Not all
these hand-held poses will be successful: 180° on a plate asks

for open-heartedness as well as skill. As I said, we were in a house
behaving like a short story, the clouds were perfect and round.

Seen

Last night I popt upon a Comet. It is visible to the naked eye
between Famalhaut and β Ceti ... Decr. 9, 1805
— William Herschel, letter to his sister Caroline

The house is rapt, an audience gripped
        by the grainy close-up shot

of the new face in town, its frown
        and four o'clock shadow, the smoke

—the focus is intimate, stark, summoning
        brilliance out of the darkening space

beyond the frame, the thin beam of light,
        sprinkling a fine film of dust

in the viewers' eyes that's easily taken
        for tears. The lingering look

is being invented, the hand-held pan,
        the bright-haired profile, the pores

like tiny craters on the skin of a man
        in the moon. Between him and us

all distance has disappeared, we're thrilled by
        the flicker and hiss, his fire and ice.

Comet Sweeper

In another dream, it's I who am flying. Wherever you look
there are people in pain, suffering unseen intrusions,

eavesdroppers, radiations. All those telescopes, leaking light
too faint and faraway for warmth. She sits too long

grinding glass for mirrors while I levitate around the room
at head height, reading over her rheumaticky shoulder some notes

she made in the small hours, laborious almanacks of unworthy stars.
I was surprised, expecting a more ostentatious repertoire.

Her astral body, often visible in a domestic role,
is really a dwarf elliptical galaxy made of dust and helium.

Nonetheless, what with the empty distances there and back,
their tempi of slow foxtrot and delirium, it was the eight comets

more than the unwritten autobiography that made her name:
those scene-stealers of flare-up, tail-plumes, flight-path too near Earth.

Fairchild's Mule

A dried specimen of the first artificial hybrid was presented by
Thomas Fairchild, a London gardener, to the Royal Society in 1726.

To be suddenly wide-awake
sowing leaf-shadows
in the moonlit hours.

To attend.

To wait red-eyed
in the gold mist of the city's dawn
for the opening of the flowers.

Under the breath, to say
a prayer for the soul.

To steady the hand.

With a feather
to harvest the pollen-grains,

brushing only the topmost tips
of the buttery stamens.
Sweet william. Then by feel

with the forefinger and thumb of the left hand
to find the gillyflower's pistil

and hold it in the fullness of light.

To marry pollen to stigma.
Not to know, this glorious morning,

the seed can never come true.

Nebula

William realized that ... we live in a biological universe.
— Michael Hoskin, *Discoverers of the Universe,* 2011

We are made of stars,
    stars that are born, grow and die,
        we are short fiction read aloud

in an old dark house
    where moonlight is spilled
        blue as breast-milk and a clock

is counting the seconds a woman
    takes to climb up and down the stairs
        with her catalogue of hurt feelings

and in her glass eye the ghosts
    of far objects, small lives untouched
        and numberless, aching to be told.

Dark Matter

Sometimes when I am alone | in the dark, & the universe reveals yet |
another secret, I say the names | of my long, lost sisters, forgotten |
in the books that record | our science –
— Siv Cedering, *Letter from Caroline Herschel*, 1986

There were evenings when what was held here
    trembling like glass seemed an almost impossible
music, a life to be lived between the usual interference
    of mirrors and the static of abstraction, savage, lustrous

that left only a dust of dead stars, fast-decaying by morning.
    Such slow news from a far-away past, uncannier
than marks on papyrus, nenuphars, tomb-pollen:
    work in the dark of the kind a deep-sky astronomer

must take in her stride. Sleepless and straining her eyes
    at the small print, she tries to decode the scrolls of unrolling
data, their automatic re-writing, like the tiny librettoed backs
    of seed packets or swarms of black dots on a bee-line

for the hive of the sun. She yawns. Stargazer, world-watcher.
    Auscultator of the celestial pulse, heartbeat of light.

Sunshine Recorder

horas non numero nisi serenas

for Malcolm

There are no moving parts. The sky's a stopped clock,
tiny aeroplanes pinned like silver brooches on a blue swathe,
as if we're lying on our backs in a lost work by Alfred Wallis

of upturned fields, goggle-eyed stone houses. The sun
will burn a white hole in the sea before the paint can dry,
the sea will swallow the lighthouse, the toppling lighthouse

will escape as a golden bird over the smoking roofs
and in the kneeling valley the colours will go out one by one.
But you my love and I will measure only the cloudless hours.

Warbler

The birds flew off, having memorized from him
Their versions of song.
— Peter Redgrove, *Orpheus Dies*, 1999

To be seen at Mr Johnston's Wig Ware-Rooms:
The inimitable master Jemmy Closong
who is no more than eleven Years of Age. –
This Youth surprisingly imitates (without the Help of any Instrument)
to very great Perfection, the Notes or Songs of the following Birds,
viz. the Brown Linnet, the Blackbird,
the Sky Lark, ascending and descending,
the Robin Redbreast as at the Appearance of Day in a Winter's Morning,
the Thrush, and several others too tedious to mention.

He like the rest of the wise men grew up in earshot
of diminutive grain-eaters and black-capped dung-sifters

who migrated to town with ironmongers, bone-crushers,
gin-sellers and all the terraced-villa-dwellers with their fat-balls

and bird-feeders; redbreasts, greenfinches, filchers
of pilled wool from washing-machine filters lined their homes

in hedges the length of Acacia Avenue, sat on the fence-posts,
sang in his head.

O sweet Canada, Canada, Canada,
birdsong was earth seen from the air.

Whilst holding the wood part in one hand, twist the two parts together,
the way you would turn a key in a door lock.

One day it just stopped, the passerine chatter of nut hatch,
chiff chaff, yellow hammer (though at first he couldn't hear

the white-throated, fly-catching, night-jarring silence they made)
and only the old hard backed dictionaries could explain

pee wit or cuckoo, quack-quack
and cock-a-doodle-do.

'Tee-rew tee-rew tee-rew tee-rew,
Chew-rit chew-rit', and ever new:
'Will-will, will-will, grig-grig, grig-grig.'

A little bit of bread and no cheese, a little bit of bread and no cheese,
birdsong was the past people wished they'd been born in.

Some went mad, plugging their ears with mahjongg
and cicadas, others took to yodelling or diddling, tweeting,

hooting, scat, anything to blank out the blankness. Museums
were besieged by the mob as swanees, serinettes, fischietti, ocarinas,

dyed-feather automata with leather-bellow piston-warbles
became the must-have apps; Boccherini, Ligeti, Rossini

whose canaries, magpies and larks sounded more singable
than the real thing were the fave downloads the night

the Bird Call Lady was elected World President and Messiaen
summoned back from the dead.

Blow noiselessly.
If no sound is produced, try adjusting the shape of your hands
to better seal the gaps.

On either side of a widening river a man and his shadow
are putting thumb and finger between their remaining teeth

and blowing the day's news at each other in a lexicon
of whistle-words, elocution of birds – fragile populations

in endangered terrain, all niceties of courtship, nest-feathering,
flower-sipping, distilling to a high-pitched cry of alarm.

Listen to my evening sing-ing-ing-ing,
birdsong unfilling the air, thinning, then thinning.

Cob Oven

Small clay house (?), first or second decade of 21st century CE ...

In days to come what will they make
    of this? That it was hands-on work
with pails of water, gobs of earth

that the sky was lit with birdsong
    that the finger-prints were human
that in those times they grew marigolds

that at some point fire was involved
    that there was a hearth or heart
(it is unclear if these were the same)

that something risen was buried here
    and burned alive, that there were rites
that there was a gathering in a garden

that there were seasons, there was grain
    (which was sometimes pronounced green)?

Census

for the National Statistician

My dreams are still at it, the royals and rough sleepers
and the secret many sitting at my table spilling coffee

on the questionnaire, inserting the small statistical errors
that conceal names and places, microdata of selves

tiptoeing in from Domesday. Counting only the people,
how many visitors are staying overnight! And have we

enough sheets for them all? Others are street-partying
through the wee grey hours, and for person 5 there is a tick

next to son or daughter. Remember to include the babies.
There is so much responsibility. (Oh but is there time

to lift your eyes from the screen, peer at the sloe blossom
pale as rice, as iced water, like a blur in the trees?) The house

I grew up in looks ordinary now but the questions read aloud
fall like mystic verse on the ear. So much responsibility,

while we go on living parted from. Do not count
anything you do barefoot as part of your paid employment,

there is a spring-like randomness in the universe's heart.
If this is not the life you meant to live, please ask

for help. We belong to the beloved. How would you
describe. How well can you speak. How long can you stay.

Notes

Organ
Dr Auzoux's papier-mâché models were designed and made as a more acceptable and accessible resource than corpses for medical students studying the workings of the human body in the mid-19th century.

Medicine Chest
The one in the epigraph is the Livingstone Medicine Chest, held in the Wellcome Collection.

Progeny
The title is an echo of Victor Frankenstein's 'hideous progeny' in Mary Shelley's novel.

Experiment
In the 1730s Stephen Gray, an amateur scientist, invented the famous 'Flying Boy' demonstration, in which a boy was suspended on silken cords and an electrical charge applied; any loose matter like chaff or pieces of paper flew up and attached itself to the boy's hands. It soon became one of the most popular entertainments performed by itinerant lecturers.

A Person is not a Landscape
Giuseppe Fiorelli, who took charge of the excavations at Pompeii in 1860, realised that the unexplained voids in the ash layer had been left by the victims' bodies – he had the cavities filled with plaster to reveal their positions at the time of death.

Mad Music
Although Mozart and Beethoven, among others, composed music to be played on the glass armonica, the instrument fell out of favour because of a rumour that it made musicians and their listeners go mad.

Sphaerotheca Pannosa
I wrote the poem while leading a series of creative writing workshops at the Chelsea Physic Garden, London, in 2010 – one dewy morning there were some beautiful table arrangements of roses, which had been left long enough to be infested with powdery mildew.

The Rose
Florence Nightingale pioneered graphical presentation of statistics, the best known being her 'Diagram of the Causes of Mortality in the Army of the East', known as the rose diagram.

Peccant Attoms
On 30 September 1811, in Paris, Frances Burney d'Arblay – Fanny Burney – underwent a mastectomy of her right breast. She was able to compose a detailed account of the operation in a letter to her sister, Esther Burney, because no effective anaesthetics were available at the time. 'Peccant attoms' would be called malignant cells in today's language, and Burney reports that her surgeons cut her deeply, radically, in order to remove all possible malignancy.

Laughing Gas
Humphry Davy cajoled his friends into participating in 'ether frolics'– breathing in large quantities of nitrous oxide – and then writing up their somatic/psychotropic experiences; though he never went on to develop its use as an anaesthetic, for example in childbirth.

Lecture
The 'visceral sublime' is a phrase in the book *Swallow: Foreign Bodies, Their Ingestion, Inspiration, and the Curious Doctor Who Extracted Them* by Mary Capello.

The Classification of Clouds

The basic idea set out by Howard – a trained pharmacist and amateur meteorologist – in his 1802 essay on cloud forms and formation was that it is possible to identify, within the complexity of changing skies, a limited number of simple categories of cloud. Howard's work had an evident influence on the Romantic artists and poets, especially the development of Constable's and Turner's paintings, Shelley's poem *The Cloud* and Goethe's lyrical sequence *In Honour of Howard*, which describes the major families of cloud-shape. Clouds are a favourite topic in modern cultural studies.

In the Realm of Dreams, the Alter Ego is Master

As their views on psychology and psychoanalytic psychotherapy diverged, the relationship between Sigmund Freud and Carl Jung broke down irretrievably – so the event recounted in the last two stanzas never happened. 'Poor Conrad' (originally the pejorative name given to peasants by the aristocracy) was how Freud and his colleagues referred to their own bodies.

Heberden's Nodes

Heberden's nodes are the hard bony enlargements of the joints closest to the ends of the fingers and toes characteristic of osteo-arthritis. William Heberden (1710–1801) was a physician who wrote three volumes of *Commentarii de morborum historia et curatione.*

Thrombus

The poem owes its beginnings to Professor Alan Bleakley of the Peninsula Medical School, Devon, for his seminar in 2006 on the nature of teamwork in emergency operating theatres.

The Fallen Angels

'And Azâzêl taught men to make swords, and knives, and shields, and breastplates, and made known to them the metals of the earth and the art of working them, and bracelets, and ornaments, and the use of antimony, and the beautifying of the eyelids, and all kinds of costly stones, and all colouring tinctures …

Semjâzâ taught enchantments, and root-cuttings, Armârôs the resolving of enchantments, Barâqîjâl taught astrology, Kôkabêl the constellations, Ezêqêêl the knowledge of the clouds, Araqiêl the signs of the earth, Shamsiêl the signs of the sun, and Sariêl the course of the moon.'— *The Book of Enoch*

The poem is dedicated to Richard Holmes, author of *The Age of Wonder: How the Romantic Generation Discovered the Beauty and Terror of Science* (Harper Press, 2008), whose influence reveals itself throughout this whole collection.

The Emperor's Mother Has Delusions
The first mechanical clock was brought to China during the Ming Dynasty – 16th century CE – by the Jesuit missionaries.

Tremor
The poem was inspired by the copper-wire model of the convoluted motion of a notional particle of earth during an earthquake, made by Professor Sekiya Seikei, *c.* 1887.

Red Sky in the Morning
Robert Fitzroy – sea-captain, pioneering metereologist and devout Christian – invited Charles Darwin to accompany him on HMS Beagle's five-year survey voyage that took in the Galapagos islands. He committed suicide on 30 April 1865.

The New Guns
The military battery at the Needles, Isle of Wight, was initially equipped with six 7-inch Armstrong rifled breech-loading guns, though William (later Lord) Armstrong himself protested that the mechanism was unsuited to heavy guns.

The Invention of Night Writing
Charles Barbier de la Serre, a captain in the French army in the early 19th century, invented a system of writing that was later adapted by Louise Braille.

Saladin

On 10 December 1881 Walter Powell, MP, Captain James Templer and Mr Agg-Gardner took off from Bath in 'Saladin', a War Office balloon; an accident close to the ground near Bridport, Dorset, resulted in Templer and Agg-Gardner falling out of the balloon basket, whilst Powell was carried out of sight, never to be seen again.

Moon Landing

'Slipstick' is engineering slang for slide rule.

Ballomania

Laetitia Sage wrote in a letter 'to a Female Friend' in 1785 that her balloon flight had made her '… infinitely better pleased than I ever was at any former event of my life'.

En Travesti

It was only when the distinguished doctor James Barry died of dysentery in 1865 that it was discovered 'he' was a woman named Mary Ann Bulkley. (S)he had the highest recovery rate with sick and wounded soldiers in the Crimean war, and in 1826 performed one of the first successful Caesarean sections. (S)he eventually rose to the rank of Inspector General in charge of military hospitals. The hey-day of the music-hall – with male impersonator acts like Vesta Tilley's still able to shock and scandalise – was half a century later.

The epigraph is a condensed version of the description of Diane Torr's 'Drag King' workshops given by Judith Halberstam in her chapter, 'Drag Kings: masculinity and performance', in *The Subcultures Reader*, edited by Ken Gelder and published by Routledge (1998, 2005).

A Sheep, a Duck and a Cockerel

The epigraph is taken from Richard Holmes' *The Age of Wonder* (see above). Colonel Joseph Kittinger holds the record for the highest, longest and fastest sky-dive, which he made in 1960.

Glass

The inspiration for the poem was a glass model of the sporangia of *Bremia Lactucae* (downy mildew) made by Dr W A R Dillon-Weston for the instruction of farmers. The poem is also inhabited by the delusion, common in the early modern period, in which sufferers believe they are turning to glass.

A Hare's Breath

The poem was inspired by seeing an image, viewed through an 18th century microscope, of a flea around whose head is a halo – the result of chromatic aberration. And of course one can't help being reminded of William Blake's engraving 'Ghost of a Flea'. (It seems no coincidence that the prevalent view of the microscope was that it led to a greater understanding of God's creation.) An internet search for 'hair's breadth' (an informal unit of length which, until the mid-20th century, was about the same as the highest resolution of microscopic measurement, about 10–5 metres) also threw up a site containing the question 'what is a "hare's breath"?'.

Cloud Camera

A cloud camera uses a fish-eye lens to take photographs of the whole sky – such techniques date from the early 20th century. As R Hill remarked in a paper for the *Quarterly Journal of the Royal Meteorological Society* in 1924, the projection of a hemisphere onto a plane cannot be accomplished without some distortion.

Comet Sweeper

'I found I was to be trained as assistant-astronomer, and by way of encouragement a Telescope adapted for 'sweeping', consisting of a Tube with two glasses such as are commonly used in a 'finder', was given to me. I was to 'sweep for comets' and I see by my journal that I began on August 22nd 1782 to write down and describe all remarkable appearances I saw in my 'sweeps', which were horizontal.' — Caroline Herschel's journal, 1783.

Dark Matter

According to Dame Jocelyn Bell Burnell (in her editor's introduction to *Dark Matter: Poems of Space*, Calouste Gulbenkian Foundation, 2008), 'only dark matter can prevent our universe from flying apart …' It was whilst working on her PhD at New Hall, Cambridge, in 1967 that Bell Burnell discovered pulsars – though it was her supervisor who was awarded the Nobel Prize.

Sunshine Recorder

The Campbell Stokes sunshine recorder is a simple device for recording the amount of sunshine at a given location. As the instrument can work only when the sun is shining and the sky is clear, it was common for recorders to bear the legend *horas non numero nisi serenas*, 'I count only the bright hours'.

Warbler

The opening section in italics is from a newspaper advertisement, *c.* 1760, on display in the Whipple Museum. The two sets of instructions (also in italics) came with toys for imitating bird-calls. The Bird Call Lady is Nicole Perretta, famed for her mimicry of birds. The old man is 'speaking' a whistled language called Silbo Gomero, now almost extinct.

Cob Oven

The poem imagines an outdoor clay oven as an exhibit in the BBC's 'A History of the World in a Hundred Objects'.

Two Rivers Press has been publishing in and about Reading since 1994.
Founded by the artist Peter Hay (1951–2003), the press continues
to delight readers, local and further afield, with its varied list of
individually designed, thought-provoking books.